4

Lehrwerk für den Englischunterricht ab Klasse 3

Pupil's Book 4

Erarbeitet von
Jasmin Brune
Daniela Elsner
Stefanie Gleixner-Weyrauch
Marion Lugauer
Sabine Schwarz

Auf der Grundlage der Ausgabe von
Martina Bredenbröcker, Jasmin Brune,
Daniela Elsner, Barbara Gleich,
Stefanie Gleixner-Weyrauch,
Simone Gutwerk, Marion Lugauer,
Sabine Schwarz

Unter Beratung von
Jane Brockmann-Fairchild

Illustriert von
Barbara Jung, Wilfried Poll,
Sandra Reckers, Andreas Fischer,
Thilo Pustlauk, Gisela Vogel

Inhalt

 pupil's CD / teacher's CD

 teacher's CD only

 Sally's task

 extra

 Work with a partner.

Work in groups.

 Write.

 Draw.

 Speak.

Rap: Welcome back to school!

Susan

Step to the left, step to the right.

Raise your  and feel alright.

Turn around and say, "That's cool!"

Welcome back to school!

Tim

Eric

Sit on your , write in the air.

Let's have fun with English.

Dance to the beat and say, "That's cool!"

Welcome back to school!

Emily

Phil

Around the classroom you must look.

Put your  on the .

Turn around and say, "That's cool!"

Welcome back to school!

Liz

1  **Listen and sing.**

2  **Act out the rap.**

Sing and record.

Let's play a board game!

Roll the dice. Take turns.

Red number:
Do what it says
or answer the question.
If you don't know a word,
look it up in your dictionary.
If you can't, miss a turn.

The winner is the first
to reach finish.

START

1 2 3 — Name 3 pets.

6 — Name the days of the week.

9 — Bend your knees.

13 — Have you got brothers or sisters?

17 — What's your favourite colour?

20 — Stand on one leg for 30 seconds.

23 — How do you feel today?

26 — Count from 1–12.

28 — What's your telephone number?

31 — When's your birthday?

34 — What's your favourite toy?

1 Play in groups (2–5).

Sing a birthday song.

79 80

FINISH

50 51 52

53

49 54

Say a rhyme or sing a song.

48 55

47 What's your hobby? 56

Shake your arms and legs.

76

77

78

46 75

45 57 74

What do you eat for breakfast?

What's the name of your best friend?

44 58 73

Show me your socks. What colour are they?

43 59 72

42 60 71

Do you like ketchup on your cornflakes?

41 Name 5 different kinds of fruit. 61 70

What's the weather like today?

40 62 69

39 63 68

38 Who is this? 64 Name 5 things in your classroom. 67

37 65 66

2 Do the English rally.

100 little kangaroos are sitting on Big Ben

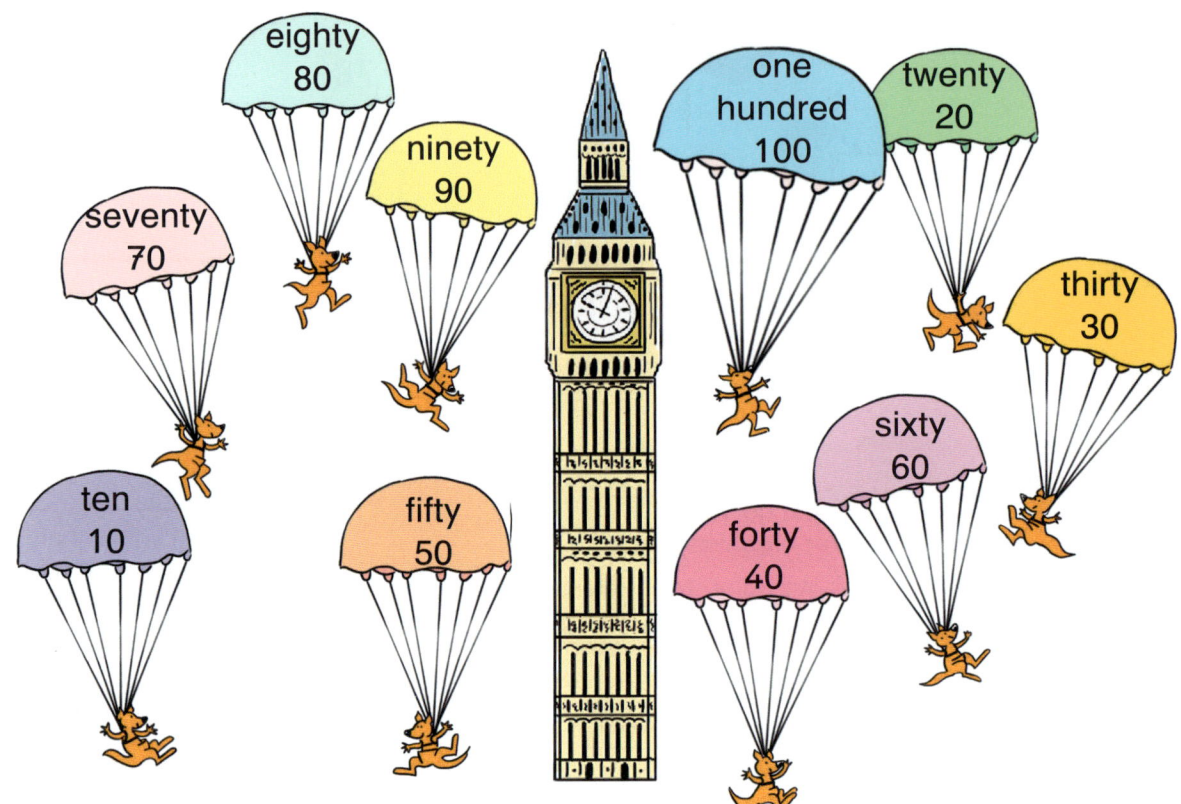

100 little kangaroos are sitting on Big Ben.
10 of them just jump away. How many are there then?

90 little kangaroos are sitting on Big Ben.
10 of them just jump away. How many are there then?

80 little kangaroos are sitting on Big Ben.
10 of them just jump away. How many are there then?

70 little kangaroos are sitting on Big Ben.
10 of them just jump away. How many are there then?
...

twen**ty**, thir**ty**, for**ty**, ...

1  **Listen and say the chant.**

2 **Sing the song faster and faster.**

Sing and record.

Gavin the ghost

Gavin is angry. He has got the hiccups ...

Hic! Hic!

... in the kitchen ...

Hic! Hic!

Can you stop my hiccups?

Drink a glass of water. Don't breathe.

Hic! Hic!

... in the living room ...

Stand on your head. Sing a song.

Head and shoulders, ...

Hic! Hic!

... in the bathroom ...

Hold your nose. Count from 20 to 30.

Hic!

Hic!

20, 21, 22, 23, ...

... in the bedroom ...

Let's play hide-and-seek!

Gavin looks for his family.

Hic! Hic!

Gavin sits on the stairs.

Boo!

Aargh!

Hooray! My hiccups are gone!

Hic!

1 Listen and read.

2 Act out the story.

The crazy house

The door is too small.

The chair is too big.

The bed is too small.

The sofa is just right.

1 Look at the pictures. What's wrong?
Tell your partner.

2 Design your own crazy house.
Present it to your class.

In my crazy house there is …

There **is** 1 …
There **are** 2/3/4 …

Let's make Sally's sandwich!

You need:
bread
ketchup
butter
a tomato
a cucumber
an egg
ham
cheese
lettuce

Take a slice of bread.
Put it on a plate.

Spread butter and ketchup on it.

Cut the tomato, the egg and the cucumber.
Put them on the bread.

Put some ham, cheese and lettuce on it.

Put another slice of bread on top.

Cut the sandwich in half.
Sally's sandwich is ready to eat!

1 **Look and read.**

2 **Make your own sandwich:**
What do you want to put on your sandwich? Make a shopping list in your group. Talk about who wants to bring the bread, ham, …

Let's have lunch

It's lunchtime

Many people eat hamburgers at a diner.

This is a typical American hot dog stand.

You can find many fish and chips shops in England.

FOOD		DRINKS	
pizza	£1	orange juice	£1
hamburger	£1	coke	£1
salad with ham	£1.20	lemonade	£1
tomato soup	£1	tea	£1
cheese sandwich	£1	coffee	£1
chicken sandwich	£1.30	water	£1

Can I help you?

That's £ …, please.

Yes. I'd like …

How much is it?

1 Look and read.

2 Listen to the text.
What do Emily and Phil order?

3 Now you are in a restaurant.
Act out the scene.

Can I help you?   I'd like …

Make a video.

Hobbies

riding a horse	riding a bike	playing the guitar
reading books	ice skating	playing the piano	snowboarding
playing tennis	playing football	swimming

1 💬 **Look at the children.**
What are their hobbies?
Eric's hobby is … / Emily's hobbies are … /

2 ✏️ **Write a word web with hobby words.**
Use your dictionary.

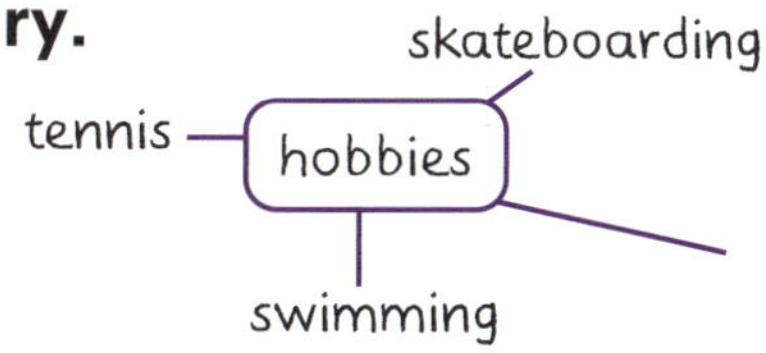

skateboarding
tennis — hobbies
swimming

My hobb**y is** …
My hobb**ies are** …

3 💬 **What's your hobby?**
Show your photos and tell your class:
My hobby is …

The interview

1 💬 **Ask your partner.**

Can you ...?

Yes, I can.

No, I can't.

Can you

play football

sing a song

play the guitar

ride a skateboard

inline skate

?

2 💿 **Listen to the interview with a sports star.**

Dirk likes playing basketball.

I can sing.
My hobby is sing**ing**.

3 🦊 **Do your own interview.**

Make a video.

Emily's day

At 8 o'clock I get up and have breakfast.

School begins at 9 o'clock.

At half past 12 I have lunch.

At 3 o'clock I go home.

At quarter to 4 I do my homework.

At 5 o'clock I call my friends and we play football.

At quarter past 6 I have dinner.

At 8 o'clock I read a book or watch TV.

At 9 o'clock I go to bed. Good night!

1 Listen, look and read.

2 What about your day? Tell your partner:
In the morning …
In the afternoon …
In the evening / At night …

 And what do you do at a weekend? Use your dictionary.

> MY WEEKEND
> On Saturday, I get up at …
> On Sunday, I …

At the same time

Somewhere in the world school starts.
At the same time …

… a little cat spills a glass of lemonade …

… a shark looks for some food in the ocean …

… a baby eats some chocolate ice cream …

… a skateboard rolls down a hill …

… a father forgets
about his pancake …

… a mouse kisses a horse …

… somewhere in the world
school is over.

1 **Look and read.**

2 💬 **What else happens at the same time?**
Talk to your class.

3 🦊 **Make your own storybook.**
Use a dictionary.

I eat.
He/She/It eats.

In the supermarket

Special offer!

99 p

BISCUITS

chocolate bars

drinks

lemonade

Pay here!

bread   rolls

juice

biscuits   jam

water

coffee   tea

milk

SUPER MARKET

cheese

pineapples

butter   eggs

apples

honey

bananas

lemons

oranges

cherries

spinach

pears

1 🔴 **Listen and point.**

2 ✏️ **Make your own shopping list.**

3 👦👧 **Talk to your partner.**

Have you got cheese (ham, …)
on your shopping list?

Yes, I have.

No, I haven't.

What's for dinner?

1  Listen and point.

2 Read the text.
Practise in your group.

3 Act out the story.

Make a video.

 Dad, what's for dinner? We're hungry.

 What about sausages with mashed potatoes and peas?

 Yeah, great idea!

 We've got sausages. Please, go to the supermarket and buy some potatoes and peas … And get some jam for breakfast.

 Okay, let's go.

 Make a shopping list.

 But Dad! We're clever! We don't need a shopping list!

 Hello, kids! I've got some great chocolate. Would you like to try it?

 Yummy! Great! Thank you!

 Now let's buy what we need. Tomatoes, peas and jam.

 Hello, kids! I've got some great strawberries. Would you like to try them?

 Yummy! Great! Thank you!

 Now let's buy what we need. We've got the tomatoes. We need cheese and jam.

 Hello, kids! I've got some great lemonade. Would you like to try it?

 Yummy! Great! Thank you!

 Now let's buy what we need. We've got the tomatoes and cheese. We need some ham.

 Look dad, we've got everything. Tomatoes, cheese and ham.

 Tomatoes, cheese and ham? But we need potatoes, peas and jam! I told you to make a shopping list, you clever kids!

 Oh sorry! What's for dinner now?

 Hm, let's make a pizza with tomatoes, ham and cheese.

 Great! We don't need a shopping list. We've got a clever dad.

Jack and the beanstalk

1 💿 **Listen, look and point.**

2 🦊 **Act out the story.**

Let's act it out!

Reading and learning the story

Painting the background

Making the music

Telling and acting the story

Practising the story

Performing the story

Flying to London

1 **Look and read.**

The red double-decker bus is famous in London.

The traditional London taxi is black. You drive on the left-hand side of the road.

The underground in London is one of the oldest in the world.

There are lots of ferries on the River Thames.

2 **Look at the photos and read.**

⭐ **Where do you live? What can you see in your town? Talk to your partner.**

Detective Brighthead

1 🔴 **Listen to the story and look at the pictures.**

⭐ **Which vehicles do you take?**
I take the …

The clever tortoise

 Listen, look and read.

The five-minute zoo game

Start

Play with a partner.

Play for five minutes.

Roll the dice.

Take turns.

The winner is the player who has got the most points.

Move in any direction.

Animal picture:
Name the animal = 1 point.
Name the animal and describe it = 2 points.

Snack stop: You must pay. Miss a turn.

Crocodile: Bad luck! You lose 1 point.

At the doctor's

I'm sick. My ear hurts. I've got an earache.

DOCTOR C. ROC

Next, please!

I'm fine, thanks.

I'm sick. My neck hurts. I've got a neckache.

DOCTOR C. ROC

Next, please!

I'm fine, thank you.

I'm sick. My head hurts. I've got a headache.

DOCTOR C. ROC

Next, please!

I'm fine, thanks.

I'm sick. My back hurts. I've got a backache.

DOCTOR C. ROC

Next, please!

I'm fine, thank you.

?

1 **Look and read.**

2 **Why do the animals run away? Guess.**

3 **Act out the story.**

Make a video.

The inline skating accident

Next, please!

My leg hurts so much. And my hand hurts, too.

What's the matter?

An apple a day keeps the doctor away.

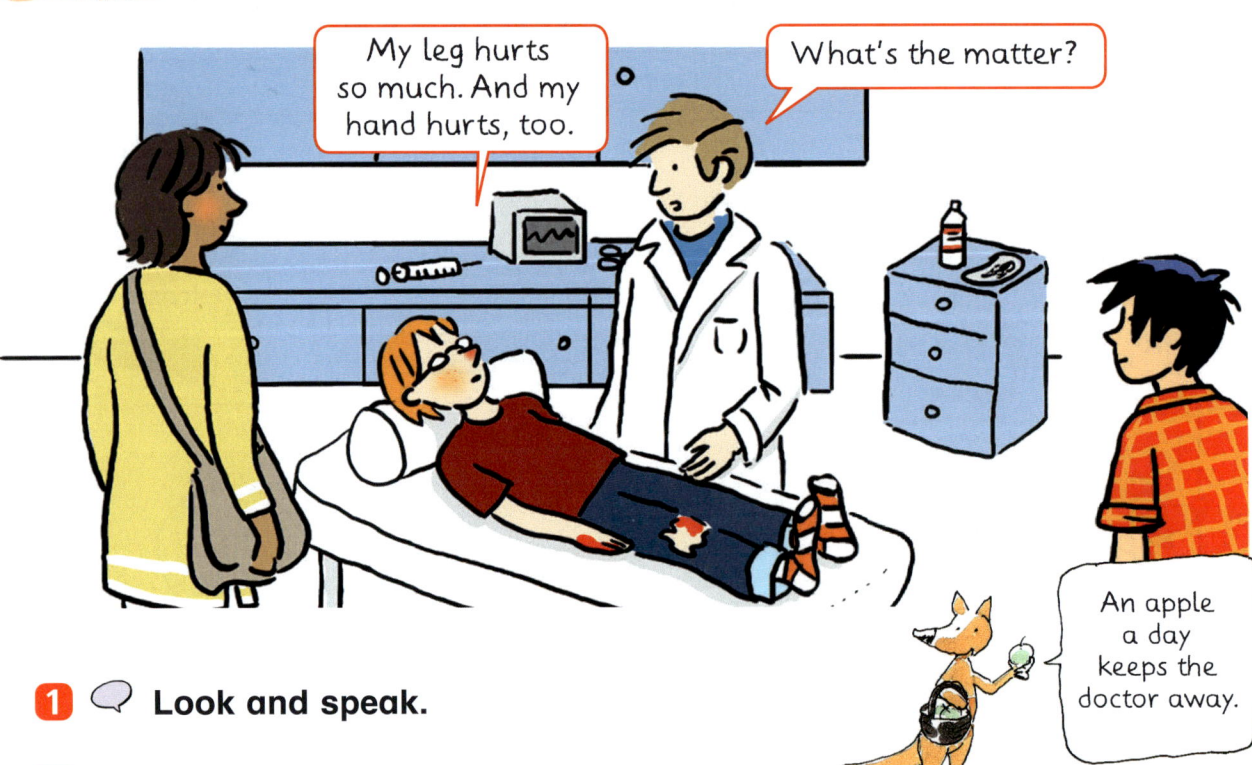

1 💬 **Look and speak.**

2 ✏️ **Look at the people in the waiting room.**
What's the matter?
Write a sentence about each patient.
The boy has got a headache …

headache   neckache
earache   backache

First aid

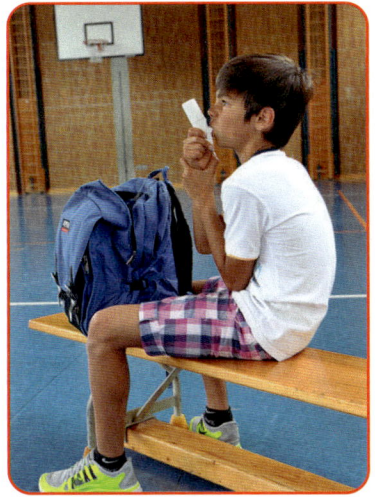

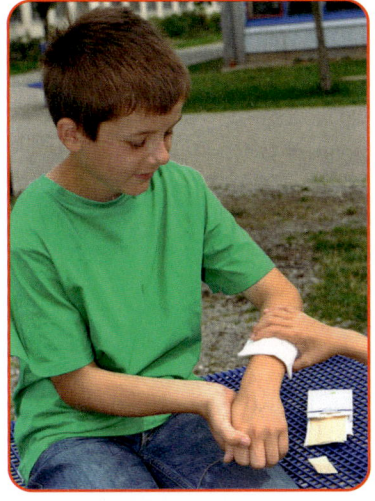

Here is what you can do

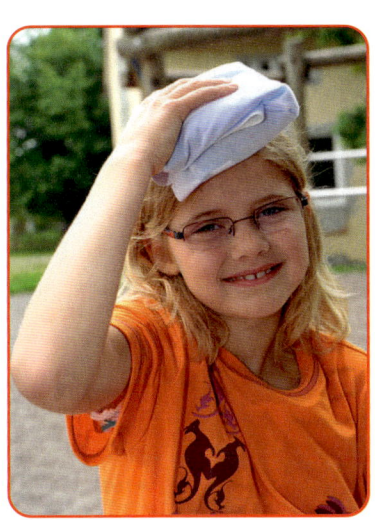

Sit down.

Get your medicine.

Cool it.

Get a plaster
or a bandage.

Put pressure
on the wound.

Call 112.

I'll help you!

1 🔘 **Listen and point.**

2 👥 **What can you do? Tell your partner.**

3 🦘 **Make a first-aid book.**

Going to Scotland

Sally and the Loch Ness Monster

A photo of the Loch Ness Monster!

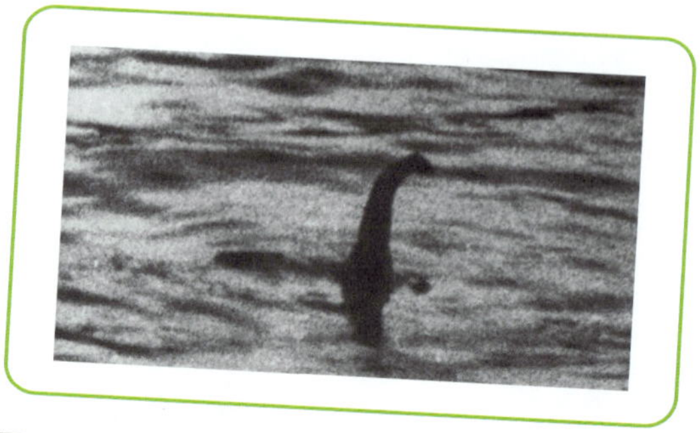

Welcome!

Hello!

Where is Nessie?

Where is Nessie?

Goodbye, Uncle!

Robert, Sally, look at this photo!

There's Nessie in the lake!

1 Listen, look and point.

2 Read and tell the story.

3 Draw your own Nessie. Describe her to your class.

A holiday trip to Scotland

Visit Edinburgh Castle.

Enjoy the Highland Games.

I want to go to a castle.

I want to see the Highland Mountains and go fishing.

I want to visit the Highland Games.

I want to go to the sea.

And we all want to see Nessie!

Come to the Seabird Centre.

Go for a walk in the Highland Mountains.

Find Nessie in Loch Ness.

1 💬 **Look and speak:**
Mr Brown wants to see …

Find information on the Internet.

2 🦊 **Plan your own holiday trip to Scotland.**

Scottish dance

Left foot, right foot, up and down and then take your part – ner and be – gin a – gain.

Right foot, left foot up and down and then clap your hands and stop!

Today I'm wearing my kilt.

1  **Listen, sing and dance.**

2 **Do the rallies.**

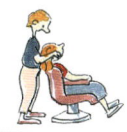

What do you want to be?

shop assistant

hairdresser

teacher

football player

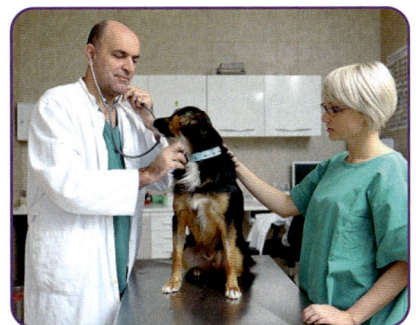

vet

doctor

policewoman

I want to be a superstar!

1 **Listen and point.**

 What do you want to be? Use your dictionary.
I want to be a …

My jobs

I have to help in the garden.

I have to tidy my room.

I have to do
my homework.

I have to feed the cat.

I have to make my bed.

I have to walk the dog.

I have to help
in the kitchen.

Do you have
to tidy your room?

I have to tidy
my pouch!

1 Look and read.

2 💬 **What do you have to do?**
I have to …

It's OK to be different!

We are all different.

Some kids have blond hair
and light coloured skin.

Some kids have dark hair
and dark coloured skin.

Some kids wear glasses
that help them to see.
Some kids talk with an accent
that's different from me.

Some kids get to ride
in cool looking wheelchairs.
They take the ramp while others
take the stairs.

Remember, it's OK to be different.
It's OK to be you!
You were made to be different.
You were made to be ...**YOU**.

1 Listen, look and read the story.

2 What makes you different? Tell your class.

We all live in the same world

Hola!

Juanita

Bonjour!

Jacqueline

Ciao!

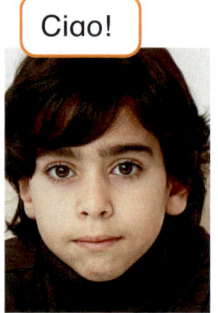

Paolo

Hello!

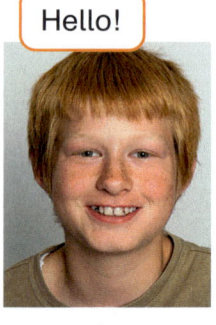

Thomas

Hallo!

Maria

Merhaba!

Güler

Jassu!

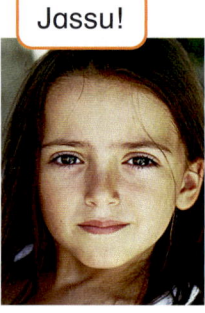

Dimitra

Priwjet!

Sergej

He/She is from …	He/She speaks …
England	English
France	French
Germany	German
Greece	Greek
Italy	Italian
Russia	Russian
Spain	Spanish
Turkey	Turkish

But we all laugh in the same language.
We all like to sing and play.
We all live in the same world,
no matter where we're from.

1 **Where are the children from?
What language do they speak?**

Jacqueline is from France.
She speaks French.

2 **Listen and sing.**

What's the word for Hello **in
different languages? Make a list.**

Look it up on
the Internet.

This is me!

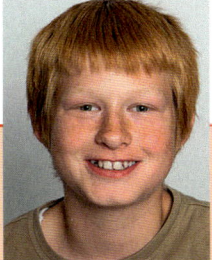

My name is Thomas.
I live in London.
I'm 9 years old.
I speak English and German.
I've got 2 sisters,
Mary and Liz.
I like playing football.
I want to be a teacher.
My favourite food is
chicken and chips and
chocolate ice cream.

My name is
Güler.
I'm from
Turkey.
I'm 10 years old.
I speak Turkish and English.
My hobbies are swimming
and riding a horse.
My favourite pet is a cat.

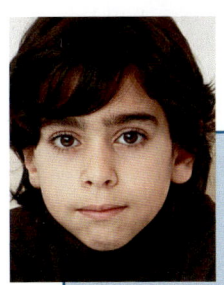

My name is Paolo.
I'm from Italy.
I'm 9 years old.
I speak Italian and English.
I've got a dog. His name is Rocco.
My brother Enrico is 11 years old,
my sister Stella is 7 years old.
I can play the piano.
I love pizza with ham and strawberries.

What's your name?
Where are you from?
When's your birthday?

1 🎵 **Listen and read.**

2 🦊 **Write about yourself. Present your text to your class.**
My name is ... I live in ... I speak ...

Messages from all over the world

Canada

Ireland

Great Britain

United States of America

CAUTION CROSSING AT NIGHT

Hi Noah,
Greetings from ⬭.
I'm having a great weekend
at the beach.
There are lots of sheep
and kiwis.
Yours,
Henry

Dear Sarah,
Greetings from ⬤.
I'm on a safari with
my family.
I'm taking lots of pictures
of elephants and zebras.
It's great!
Yours,
Anne

Hello Ravi,
I'm on a super holiday in
I like Dublin and the castles here.
See you soon,
Mary

India

New message   — ⬈ ✕

Aw: Greetings
An: Jill

Dear Jill,
Greetings from .
I'm on a camping trip. I'm having lots of fun.
Hope I don't meet a grizzly bear!
Yours, Harry

≡ A ⬚ ☺ 🖼 ☆ 🗑   send

South Africa

Australia

New Zealand

1 ✏ **In which countries do people speak English? Make a list.**

2 **Read the messages. Where are they from?**

Guy Fawkes Day – Bonfire Night

Penny for the guy!

5th November
Guy Fawkes Day

fireworks at night

bonfire at night

1 💬 **Look at the pictures. Read the text.**

2 💿 **Listen to the story about Guy Fawkes.**

⭐ **Do you know other festivals with fireworks or bonfires?**

　　　　CD 2.22

Thanksgiving today

Mum gets up at 6 o'clock in the morning.
She puts the turkey into the oven.
The turkey takes five hours to cook.

At 12 o'clock my family comes to our house. We have our Thanksgiving dinner: turkey with potatoes, carrots, corncobs and pumpkin pie.

In the afternoon we go to the Thanksgiving parade.

In the evening we watch the football match on TV.

1 🔴 **Listen to the story of Carol's Thanksgiving.**

2 Look at the photos and read.

A turkey is a funny bird, his head goes wobble, wobble. And he knows just one word: "Gobble, gobble, gobble!"

A story about the first Thanksgiving

The first Thanksgiving

1 💿 **Listen to the story about the first Thanksgiving.**

2 💬 **Look at the picture. What can you see?**

> pumpkin   corncobs   potatoes   beans   tomatoes
> turkey   Native Americans   settlers   fishing

Find information on the Internet.

3 💬 **What do you know about the Native Americans?**

Come to the USA!

A cowboy in Texas shows how he works.

The Statue of Liberty is in New York.

The Mississippi is a very long river.
You can take a ride on a steamboat.

The President of the USA lives in the
White House in Washington, D.C.

The Grand Canyon National Park is in
Arizona. The views are great!

In San Francisco, California, cable cars
go up and down the roads.

1 **Look at the photos.**

2 💬 **What do you know about the USA?**

Find information on
the Internet.

3 **Make a poster, a collage or a report
about the USA. Present it to your class.**

Father Christmas in Australia

It's too hot! The reindeer can't pull the sleigh.

Can we help you?

Stop! Stop!

I've got a good idea!

Merry Christmas!

1 **Listen and point.**

3 **Act out the story.**

2 **Read.**

 Write a Christmas card.

The five days of Christmas

kookaburra

On the first day of Christmas
my true love sent to me
a  in a gum tree.

On the second day of Christmas
my true love sent to me

two small

and a  in a gum tree.

koala

cockatoo

On the third day of Christmas
my true love sent to me

three  ,

two small …

On the fourth day of Christmas
my true love sent to me

four  ,

three …

crocodile

kangaroo

On the fifth day of Christmas
my true love sent to me

five  ,

four …

1  **Look at the photos. Listen and sing.**

2 **Write word cards for a Christmas bingo.**
sleigh, reindeer, stocking, present, star,
Christmas tree, winter, cold, snowy…

G'day!

Let's go to Australia!

Sydney is the biggest city.

A road train is a very long truck.

Ayers Rock is a big flat rock.

At the Great Barrier Reef you can see coral and coloured fish.

An Australian Aborigine is playing the didgeridoo.

1 🔘 **Listen, look and point.**

2 **Read the text.**
Find the correct photo.

3 **Find more information about Australia.**

Look it up on the Internet.

⭐ **Look and draw your own traffic sign.**

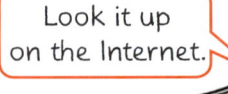

Next 92 km

Let's make an Easter bunny mosaic card!

You need:
coloured eggshells
cardboard
a pencil
glue
scissors

Funny little bunny
goes hop, hop, hop!
Funny little bunny,
please stop, stop, stop!

Break the eggshells
into small pieces.

Draw your Easter bunny
on the cardboard. Cut it out.

Glue the eggshells on your
Easter bunny.

Glue your Easter bunny
onto the cardboard. Write an
Easter greeting on your card.

1 Look and read. Make your own Easter card.
Write "Happy Easter!" on your card.

2 Can you say "Happy Easter!" in other languages?

Rules

There **is** 1 …
There **are** 2/3/4 …

I **like** swimming.
He/She **likes** swimming.

1 knife – 2 kni**ves**
1 glass – 2 glass**es**

I make **my** bed.
You make **your** bed.

I can sing.
My hobby is
sing**ing**.

I eat.
He/She/It eat**s**.

I've got **an e**arache.
I've got **a b**ackache.

Tom **k**angaroo
Scotland **u**ncle
England **b**ook

 Numbers and time
Zahlen und Uhrzeiten

eleven   elf
twelve   zwölf
thirteen   dreizehn
fourteen   vierzehn
fifteen   fünfzehn
sixteen   sechzehn
seventeen   siebzehn
eighteen   achtzehn
nineteen   neunzehn
twenty   zwanzig
thirty   dreißig
forty   vierzig
fifty   fünfzig
sixty   sechzig
seventy   siebzig
eighty   achtzig
ninety   neunzig
a/one hundred   hundert
a/one thousand   tausend

clock   Uhr
hand   (Uhr-)Zeiger
(to) set   stellen

What time is it?   Wie spät ist es?

It's 1 (2, 3 ...) o'clock.
Es ist 1 (2, 3 ...) Uhr.

It's quarter past 1 (2, 3 ...).
Es ist Viertel nach 1 (2, 3 ...).

It's half past 1 (2, 3...).
Es ist halb 2 (3, 4 ...).

It's quarter to 2 (3, 4 ...).
Es ist Viertel vor 2 (3, 4 ...).

 At home   Zu Hause

attic   Speicher
bathroom   Badezimmer
bedroom   Schlafzimmer
castle   Schloss, Burg
cellar   Keller
garden   Garten
hiccups   Schluckauf
kitchen   Küche
living room   Wohnzimmer
stairs   Treppen
toilet   Toilette, WC

bed   Bett
chair   Stuhl
furniture   Möbel
just right   genau richtig
lamp   Lampe
shelves   Regal
sofa   Sofa
table   Tisch
too big   zu groß
too small   zu klein
wardrobe   Schrank

Where is ...? – He/She/It is in the ...
Wo ist ...? – Er/Sie/Es ist im / in der ...

Is he/she/it in the ...? –
Yes, he/she/it is. / No, he/she/it isn't.
Ist er/sie/es im / in der ...? – Ja. / Nein.

 Let's have lunch   Lasst uns
Mittag essen

bread   Brot
cheese   Käse
chicken and chips   Hühnchen mit
Pommes frites

cucumber   Gurke

fish and chips   Fisch mit
Pommes frites

ham   Schinken

hamburger   Hamburger

hot dog   Hotdog

ketchup   Ketchup

lettuce   Kopfsalat

lunch   Mittagessen

mustard   Senf

pizza   Pizza

salad   Salat

sandwich   Sandwich

sausage with mashed potatoes
Würstchen mit Kartoffelbrei

soup   Suppe

spaghetti   Spaghetti

tomato   Tomate

cup   Tasse

fork   Gabel

glass   Glas

knife – knives   Messer –
Messer (Plural)

plate   Teller

spoon   Löffel

Can I help you? – I'd like ..., please.
Kann ich dir/euch/Ihnen helfen? –
Ich hätte gerne ..., bitte.

Would you like something to drink? –
I'd like a glass of ..., please.
Hättest du / Hätten Sie gerne etwas
zu trinken? – Ich hätte gerne ein Glas ...,
bitte.

That's ... pounds. – Here you are.
Das macht ... Pfund. – Hier, bitte.

 Hobbies and sports
Hobbys und Sportarten

basketball   Basketball

book   Buch

(to) do   tun, machen

fun   Spaß

great   großartig

hobby – hobbies   Hobby – Hobbys

ice skating   Schlittschuhfahren

interview   Interview

(to) love   sehr gerne mögen, lieben

okay   in Ordnung, OK

(to) play football   Fußball spielen

(to) play the piano/the guitar
Klavier/Gitarre spielen

(to) read   lesen

reporter   Reporter

(to) ride a horse   ein Pferd reiten

(to) ride a bike
Fahrrad fahren

(to) run   rennen, laufen

snowboarding   snowboarden

sports   Sport(arten)

sports star   Sportstar

(to) swim   schwimmen

tennis   Tennis

What's your hobby? – My hobby is ... /
My hobbies are ... / I like ...
Was ist dein Hobby? –
Mein Hobby ist ... / Meine Hobbys
sind ... / Ich mag gerne ...

Do you like ...? – Yes, I do. /
No, I don't.   Magst du ...? – Ja. / Nein.

Can you play ...? – Yes, I can. /
No, I can't.   Kannst du ... spielen? –
Ja. / Nein.

My day   Mein Tagesablauf

morning   Morgen, Vormittag
afternoon   Nachmittag
evening   Abend
night   Nacht

at the same time   zur selben Zeit
breakfast   Frühstück
(to) brush   bürsten
(to) call   rufen, anrufen
dinner   Abendessen
(to) get up   aufstehen
(to) go to bed   zu Bett gehen
(to) go to school   zur Schule gehen
(to) learn   lernen
lunch   Mittagessen
(to) meet   treffen
(to) play   spielen
time   Zeit
(to) watch TV   fernsehen

What do you do at … o'clock?
Was machst du (normalerweise)
um … Uhr?

I do my homework.   Ich mache
meine Hausaufgaben.

 Shopping   Einkaufen

apple   Apfel
biscuit   Keks
cheese   Käse
chocolate   Schokolade
chocolate bar   Schokoriegel
egg   Ei
ham   Schinken
honey   Honig
ice cream   Eis(creme)
lemonade   Limonade

lollipop   Lutscher
milk   Milch
orange   Orange
orange juice   Orangensaft
peas   Erbsen
spinach   Spinat

book shop   Buchladen
cart   Einkaufswagen
cash register   Kasse
clothes shop   Kleiderladen
computer shop   Computerladen
music shop   Musikgeschäft
products   Produkte, Erzeugnisse
restaurant   Restaurant
shelf – shelves   Regalbrett – Regal
shoe shop   Schuhgeschäft
shop assistant   Verkäufer
shop   Geschäft, Laden
shopping bag   Einkaufstasche
shopping centre   Einkaufszentrum
shopping list   Einkaufsliste
sports shop   Sportgeschäft
supermarket   Supermarkt
sweets shop   Süßwarenladen
toy shop   Spielwarenladen
(to) try on   anprobieren

Have you got … on your shopping list?
Hast du … auf deiner Einkaufsliste?

In the supermarket (book shop …)
I can buy …   Im Supermarkt
(Buchladen …) kann ich … kaufen.

Excuse me, please. Where can
I buy …? – Go to … It's on the … floor.
Entschuldigen Sie, bitte.
Wo kann ich … kaufen? – Gehe /
Gehen Sie zu … Das ist im … Stock.

Words

Hello, can I help you? – Yes, please.
I'd like … Hallo, kann ich dir/Ihnen
helfen? – Ja, bitte. Ich hätte gerne …

It's perfect / too big.
Es ist perfekt / zu groß.

How much is it? – It's …
Was kostet das? – Das macht …

Here you are. Hier, bitte.

I have to buy … Ich muss … kaufen.

What do you need? – I need …
Was brauchst du? – Ich brauche …

Jack and the beanstalk
Jack und die Bohnenranke

apple pie Apfelkuchen

beanstalk Bohnenranke

blood Blut

castle Schloss, Burg

(to) climb (up/down) (hinauf/hinab)
klettern

Englishman Engländer

fairy tale Märchen

giant Riese

(to) grow wachsen

(to) live leben

magic bean Zauberbohne

new neu

(to) sell verkaufen

(to) smell riechen

Yummy! Lecker!

 ### Transport Verkehrsmittel

boarding pass Bordkarte

car Auto

clockmaker Uhrmacher

detective Detektiv

(double-decker) bus
(Doppeldecker-)Bus

(to) drive fahren

famous berühmt

ferry Fähre

left-hand traffic Linksverkehr

map Landkarte, Stadtplan

museum Museum

old – oldest alt – älteste(r, s)

plane Flugzeug

station Bahnhof / Station / Haltestelle

taxi Taxi

thief Dieb

train Zug

underground U-Bahn

How can I get from … to …?
Wie kann ich von … nach …
gelangen?

You can take the …
Du kannst / Sie können den (die, das) …
nehmen.

Let's take the …
Lass(t) uns den (die, das) … nehmen.

I take the … / I go by … Ich nehme …

I'm sorry! Es tut mir leid!

Go right / left / straight ahead.
Geh / Gehen Sie rechts / links /
geradeaus.

Wild animals Wildtiere

big groß

(to) bite beißen

clever schlau

(to) climb klettern

dangerous gefährlich

elephant Elefant

fast schnell

fat dick, fett

funny komisch, lustig

giraffe Giraffe

hippo Nilpferd

jungle Dschungel

lion Löwe

long lang

monkey Affe

(to) run rennen, laufen

snake Schlange

strong stark

tail Schwanz

tall groß, hoch

tortoise (Land-)Schildkröte

trunk Rüssel

wings Flügel

zebra Zebra

zoo Zoo

(to) chew kauen

lake See

(to) pull ziehen

rope Seil, Strick

tug-of-war Tauziehen

Guess my animal: It's … /
It has got … / It can … / It lives in … /
It eats … Errate mein Tier: Es ist … /
Es hat … / Es kann … /
Es lebt in/im … / Es frisst …

At the doctor's Beim Arzt

back Rücken

backache Rückenschmerzen

(to) bleed bluten

(to) breathe atmen

(to) bump anstoßen

(to) burn sich verbrennen

(to) cool kühlen

ear Ohr

earache Ohrenschmerzen

head Kopf

headache Kopfschmerzen

neck Nacken

neckache Nackenschmerzen

(to) pinch zusammendrücken

(to) vomit sich übergeben

My ear (neck …) hurts.
Mein Ohr (Nacken …) tut weh.

I've got an earache (a neckache …).
Ich habe Ohrenschmerzen
(Nackenschmerzen …).

I'm sick. Ich bin krank.

Next, please. Der Nächste, bitte.

What's the matter (with you)?
Was fehlt dir/Ihnen?

Your leg (arm …) is broken.
Dein/Ihr Bein (Arm …) ist gebrochen.

Cool it. Kühle es.

Get your medicine.
Hole deine Medizin.

Get a plaster or a bandage.
Hole ein Pflaster oder einen Verband.

Put pressure on the wound.
Übe Druck auf die Wunde aus.

Call 112.   Rufe 112 an.

 Going to Scotland
Nach Schottland reisen

castle   Schloss, Burg
(to) discuss   besprechen
(to) go fishing   zum Angeln gehen
Highland Games   Highland Games
hill   Hügel
lake   (der) See
Loch Ness   Loch Ness
map   Landkarte, Stadtplan
mountain   Berg
Nessie   Nessie
(to) plan a trip   eine Reise planen
river   Fluss
Scotland   Schottland
sea   Meer, (die) See
(to) take a photo   ein Foto machen
(to) wait   warten

I/We want to go to ...   Ich möchte /
Wir möchten nach ... fahren.

I'd/We'd like to see ...
Ich würde / Wir würden gerne ...
sehen.

There's a ... / There are ...
Dort gibt es (ein, eine, einen) ...

On Friday (Saturday ...) we go to ...
Am Freitag (Samstag ...) fahren wir
nach ...

On Friday (Saturday ...) we visit ...

Am Freitag (Samstag ...) besichtigen
wir ...

 Jobs   Berufe

boss   Chef
bottle   Flasche
busy   beschäftigt
(to) do   tun, machen
(to) do my homework
meine Hausaufgaben machen
doctor   Arzt, Doktor
(to) feed the cat   die Katze füttern
hairdresser   Friseur
(to) help in the house/kitchen/...
im Haus / in der Küche / ... helfen
job   Beruf, Aufgabe
(to) make my bed
mein Bett machen
policewoman   Polizistin
room   Zimmer
shop assistant   Verkäufer(in)
teacher   Lehrer(in)
(to) tidy my room
mein Zimmer aufräumen
(to) turn   drehen
(to) walk the dog
den Hund ausführen
(to) work   arbeiten

What do you want to be? –
I want to be a ...
Was möchtest du werden? –
Ich möchte ... werden.

What are your jobs? – I have to ...
Welche Aufgaben hast du? –
Ich muss ...

How many in your group have
to help in the garden (kitchen …)?
Wie viele aus deiner Gruppe
müssen im Garten (in der Küche …)
helfen?

Meeting people
Menschen begegnen

accent   Betonung
different   verschieden, anders
friend   Freund, Freundin
dark coloured   dunkel
greetings   Grüße
light coloured   hell
ramp   Rampe
skin   Haut
wheelchair   Rollstuhl

Canada   Kanada
England   England
English   englisch
France   Frankreich
French   französisch
German   deutsch
Germany   Deutschland
Greece   Griechenland
Greek   griechisch
Italian   italienisch
Italy   Italien
language   Sprache
New Zealand   Neuseeland
Russia   Russland
Russian   russisch
same   gleich
South Africa   Südafrika
Spain   Spanien
Spanish   spanisch
Turkey   Türkei

Turkish   türkisch
world   Welt

Where are you from? – I'm from
England (Germany …). / I live in …
Woher kommst du? – Ich komme aus
England (Deutschland …). /
Ich lebe in …

Are you from …?
Kommst du aus …?

Do you speak English (German …)?
Sprichst du Englisch (Deutsch …)?

What languages do you speak? –
I speak …
Welche Sprachen sprichst du? –
Ich spreche …

Guy Fawkes   Guy Fawkes

bonfire   Lagerfeuer, Freudenfeuer
fireworks   Feuerwerk
Guy Fawkes Day   Jahrestag der
Guy-Fawkes-Verschwörung,
5. November

Thanksgiving Day
Erntedankfest

apple   Apfel
bean   Bohne
carrot   Karotte, Möhre
corn(cob)   Mais(kolben)
fruit   Obst, Frucht
Native American   Ureinwohner
Nordamerikas
pear   Birne
pie   Kuchen
plum   Pflaume

potato – potatoes
Kartoffel – Kartoffeln
pumpkin   Kürbis
ship   Schiff
Thanksgiving Day   Erntedankfest
Thanksgiving dinner
Erntedank-Essen
tomato – tomatoes
Tomate – Tomaten
turkey   Truthahn
vegetables   Gemüse

It's Thanksgiving Day.
Es ist Erntedankfest.

I'm thankful for ...
Ich bin dankbar für ...

Christmas in Australia
Weihnachten in Australien

first   erste(r, s)
second   zweite(r, s)
third   dritte(r, s)
fourth   vierte(r, s)
fifth   fünfte(r, s)

Aborigine   australischer Ureinwohner
capital   Hauptstadt
city   Stadt
cockatoo   Kakadu

coral   Koralle
crocodile   Krokodil
didgeridoo   Didgeridoo
kangaroo   Känguru
koala   Koala
kookaburra   Kookaburra
(to) pull   ziehen
reindeer   Rentier(e)
road train   Lastwagen
rock   Fels
sleigh   Schlitten

Merry Christmas!
Frohe Weihnachten!

Easter   Ostern

(to) break   zerbrechen
cardboard   Tonpapier, Pappe
daffodil   Narzisse, Osterglocke
Easter bunny   Osterhase
egg   Ei
eggshell   Eierschale
fireside   Kamin
flower   Blume
hill   Hügel
mountain   Berg

Happy Easter!   Frohe Ostern!